CREATIVE MANIFESTOS

OLIVER LUKE DELORIE
FOREWORD BY PETER DAWSON

CREATIVE
MANIFESTOS

INSPIRATIONAL STATEMENTS
TO CELEBRATE SELF-EXPRESSION

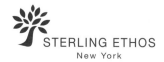

STERLING ETHOS
New York

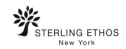

STERLING ETHOS
New York

An Imprint of Sterling Publishing Co., Inc.
1166 Avenue of the Americas
New York, NY 10036

ISBN 978-1-4549-3921-4

Distributed in Canada by Sterling
Publishing Co., Inc., c/o Canadian
Manda Group, 664 Annette Street,
Toronto, Ontario M6S 2C8, Canada

For information about custom
editions, special sales, and premium
and corporate purchases, please contact
Sterling Special Sales at 800-805-5489
or specialsales@sterlingpublishing.com.

Manufactured in Singapore

10 9 8 7 6 5 4 3 2 1

sterlingpublishing.com

For image credits, see page 186

Senior Commissioning Editor: Eszter Karpati
Design: Grade Design, London
Researcher: Susannah Jayes
Editor: Ruth Patrick
Art Director: Gemma Wilson
Publisher: Samantha Warrington

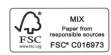

MIX
Paper from
responsible sources
FSC® C016973

CONTENTS

FOREWORD

How does one define creativity? Over the years, working within the graphic design industry and collaborating with many industrious and gifted people from a diverse range of fields and organizations, one can be certain that creativity is not the property of just the art and design movements. Creativity pervades our whole society and not only provides a platform for communicating and forming ideas, but also improves many areas of life. In my own career—spanning nearly three decades—I've been fortunate to work with people who have applied creative thinking in a variety of ways, from writing to science, engineering through fashion, in commerce, construction, finance, and photography . . . the list goes on and on. Creative thinking shapes the world we live in and the world that awaits us in the future.

Thus creativity takes many forms and does not necessarily have to be a result of working with physical elements. The impact that a conceptual idea can have on our world can be enormous. Take one of the most creative minds history has ever witnessed, acclaimed physicist Albert Einstein, who said, "The greatest scientists are artists as well." His creative thinking and documented thought processes led to his groundbreaking theory of relativity. By using a creative thinking technique called Janusian thinking (the ability to imagine two opposites or contradictory concepts existing at the same time), his theories of special relativity and general relativity enabled us to not only describe but also understand how the universe works. Contained within this book are manifestos and creative statements from a broad range of individuals from all walks of life to inspire, motivate, and enhance the creative thinker's ability. In whatever medium, and whatever future creative challenges await you, the opportunity to harness the advice from these creative manifestos will not only educate but empower your own creative thinking.

Peter Dawson
Creative Director, Grade Design

INTRODUCTION

Would you agree there are too many distractions and demands on your time, energy, and resources? Your focus and attention divide themselves between your daily responsibilities and can easily keep you from producing original work. If passion, purpose, and changing lives (even just your own) is what fuels you, you need this book in your own life.

The definition of manifesto is a public declaration of your strategies and aims. Like a tree, you need roots to grow fruit. If you want a tree bursting with creativity, your creative manifesto becomes your root—an intentional, personal, sacred agreement with yourself that will inspire, inform, and direct your artistic efforts and keep you on the beaten—or unbeaten—path to achieving your goals. Establishing your principles and perspectives on what art and process and color and sound and form and function mean to you will define the parameters of the expressive experiment, pet project, or public performance you pursue for pleasure or profit.

Let the movers and shakers featured in this book guide you; follow in their footsteps and honor them, for without their foundational precepts, all growth and innovation are directionless novelty. There are no shortcuts to wisdom via experience, education, and experimentation, so be inspired by the masters that brought the (art) world into being by studying the rough chronology of this creative concept.

Where would poetry be had the concept of Futurism not been first celebrated in myriad Italian

OPPOSITE **"Manifeste du Futurisme" (Futurist Manifesto), published in French in** *Le Figaro* **on February 20, 1909.**

MANIFESTE

DU

FUTURISME

(Pubblié par le « FIGARO » le 20 Février 1909)

Nous avions veillé toute la nuit, mes amis et moi, sous des lampes de mosquée dont les coupoles de cuivre aussi ajourées que notre âme avaient pourtant des cœurs électriques. Et tout en piétinant notre native paresse sur d'opulents tapis persans, nous avions discuté aux frontières extrêmes de la logique et griffé le papier de démentes écritures.

Un immense orgueil gonflait nos poitrines, à nous sentir debout tous seuls, comme des phares ou comme des sentinelles avancées, face à l'armée des étoiles ennemies, qui campent dans leurs bivouacs célestes. Seuls avec les mécaniciens dans les infernales chaufferies des grands navires, seuls avec les noirs fantômes qui fourragent dans le ventre rouge des locomotives affolées, seuls avec les ivrognes battant des ailes contre les murs !

Et nous voilà brusquement distraits par le roulement des énormes tramways à double étage, qui passent sursautants, bariolés de lumières, tels les hameaux en fête que le Pô débordé ébranle tout à coup et déracine, pour les entraîner, sur les cascades et les remous d'un déluge, jusqu'à la mer.

Puis le silence s'aggrava. Comme nous écoutions la prière exténuée du vieux canal et crisser les os des palais moribonds dans leur barbe de verdure, soudain rugirent sous nos fenêtres les automobiles affamées.

— Allons, dis-je, mes amis ! Partons ! Enfin la Mythologie et l'Idéal mystique sont surpassés. Nous allons assister à la naissance du Centaure et nous verrons bientôt voler les premiers Anges ! — Il faudra ébranler les portes de la vie pour en essayer les gonds et les verrous !... Partons ! Voilà bien le premier soleil levant sur la terre !... Rien n'égale la splendeur de son épée rouge qui s'escrime pour la première fois, dans nos ténèbres millénaires.

Nous nous approchâmes des trois machines renâclantes pour flatter leur poitrail. Je m'allongeai sur la mienne comme un cadavre dans sa bière, mais je ressuscitai soudain sous le volant — couperet de guillotine — qui menaçait mon estomac.

THE LAWS OF SCULPTORS

1   Always be smartly dressed, well groomed relaxed friendly polite and in complete control

2   Make the world to believe in you and to pay heavily for this privilege

3   Never worry assess discuss or criticize but remain quiet respectful and calm

4   The lord chisels still, so don't leave your bench for long

Gilbert & George, 1969

manifestos composed by Filippo Tommaso Marinetti in 1909? Until then, Italian literature bathed blissfully in "contemplative stillness." The result was a 180-degree shift in the direction of the prevailing winds that fanned flames and stoked fires with forceful, decisive declarations that would determine the future of Italian poetry. What beliefs blow your weather vane in the other direction and determine a new creative course?

Renowned architect Frank Lloyd Wright created a series of "fellowship assets" to assist his apprentices at his school, Taliesin. He not only believed that working with others should come naturally but also that one should have "an eye to see nature," "a heart to feel nature," and "the courage to follow nature." How does nature speak or feel or sound to you? What natural phenomena inspire your work?

There are no creative rules, except the ones you draft yourself. Art school brought together Gilbert Prousch and George Passmore, whose mantra "art for all" was expressed in their *Laws of Sculptors* manifesto penned in 1967. Sophisticated and refined, they believed artists should be seen and treated as the stylish, cultured, and well-mannered conduits they believed befit the creative class. Makes you think twice about how you present yourself and your art to the public, doesn't it?

Seth Godin is a well-known change agent, creative marketing genius, and entrepreneur who has penned and published many manifestos such as the *Unforgivable Manifesto*, wherein he admonishes us never to settle, for that would be unforgivable. Ever consider the idea that you have a responsibility to nurture, harness, and channel your gifts in the service of cultural (r)evolution?

Regardless of your chosen medium, you may study or adopt (or at least be inspired by) the themes,

THE STUCKISTS

(EST. 1999)

"YOUR PAINTINGS ARE STUCK, YOU ARE STUCK! STUCK! STUCK! STUCK!"

Tracey Emin

Against conceptualism, hedonism, and the cult of the ego-artist.

1 **Stuckism is the quest for authenticity.** By removing the mask of cleverness and admitting where we are, the Stuckist allows him/herself uncensored expression.

2 **Painting is the medium of self-discovery.** It engages the person fully with a process of action, emotion, thought, and vision, revealing all of these with intimate and unforgiving breadth and detail.

3 **Stuckism proposes a model of art that is holistic.** It is a meeting of the conscious and unconscious, thought and emotion, spiritual and material, private and public. Modernism is a school of fragmentation—one aspect of art is isolated and exaggerated to detriment of the whole. This is a fundamental distortion of the human experience and perpetrates an egocentric lie.

4 **Artists who don't paint aren't artists.**

5 **Art that has to be in a gallery to be art isn't art.**

6 **The Stuckist paints pictures because painting pictures is what matters.**

7 **The Stuckist is not mesmerized by the glittering prizes,** but is wholeheartedly engaged in the process of painting. Success to the Stuckist is to get out of bed in the morning and paint.

8 **It is the Stuckist's duty to explore his/her neurosis and innocence** through the making of paintings and displaying them in public, thereby enriching society by giving shared form to individual experience and an individual form to shared experience.

9 **The Stuckist is not a career artist but rather an amateur** (*amare*, Latin, to love) who takes risks on the canvas rather than hiding behind ready-made objects (e.g. a dead sheep). The amateur, far from being second to the professional, is at the forefront of experimentation, unencumbered by the need to be seen as infallible. Leaps of human endeavour are made by the intrepid individual, because he/she does not have to protect their status. Unlike the professional, the Stuckist is not afraid to fail.

10 **Painting is mysterious. It creates worlds within worlds, giving access to the unseen psychological realities that we inhabit.** The results are radically different from the materials employed. An existing object (e.g. a dead sheep) blocks access to the inner world and can only remain part of the physical world it inhabits, be it moorland or gallery. Ready-made art is a polemic of materialism.

11 **Postmodernism, in its adolescent attempt to ape the clever and witty in modern art, has shown itself to be lost in a cul-de-sac of idiocy.** What was once a searching and provocative process (as Dadaism) has given way to trite cleverness for commercial exploitation. The Stuckist calls for an art that is alive with all aspects of human experience; dares to communicate its ideas in primeval pigment; and possibly experiences itself as not at all clever!

12 **Against the jingoism of Brit Art and the ego-artist.** Stuckism is an international non-movement.

13 **Stuckism is anti "ism."** Stuckism doesn't become an "ism" because Stuckism is not Stuckism, it is stuck!

14 **Brit Art, in being sponsored by Saachis, mainstream conservatism and the Labour government, makes a mockery of its claim to be subversive or avant-garde.**

15 **The ego-artist's constant striving for public recognition results in a constant fear of failure.** The Stuckist risks failure willfully and mindfully by daring to transmute his/her ideas through the realms of painting. Whereas the ego-artist's fear of failure inevitably brings about an underlying self-loathing, the failures that the Stuckist encounters engage him/her in a deepening process, which leads to the understanding of the futility of all striving. The Stuckist doesn't strive—which is to avoid who and where you are—the Stuckist engages with the moment.

16 **The Stuckist gives up the laborious task of playing games of novelty, shock, and gimmick.** The Stuckist neither looks backward nor forward but is engaged with the study of the human condition. The Stuckists champion process over cleverness, realism over abstraction, content over void, humor over wittiness, and painting over smugness.

17 **If it is the conceptualist's wish to always be clever, then it is the Stuckist's duty to always be wrong.**

18 **The Stuckist is opposed to the sterility of the white wall gallery system and calls for exhibitions to be held in homes** and musty museums, with access to sofas, tables, chairs, and cups of tea. The surroundings in which art is experienced (rather than viewed) should not be artificial and vacuous.

19 **Crimes of education:** instead of promoting the advancement of personal expression through appropriate art processes and thereby enriching society, the art school system has become a slick bureaucracy, whose primary motivation is financial. The Stuckists call for an open policy of admission to all art schools based on the individual's work regardless of his/her academic record, or so-called lack of it.

We further call for the policy of entrapping rich and untalented students from at home and abroad to be halted forthwith.

We also demand that all college buildings be available for adult education and recreational use of the indigenous population of the respective catchment area. If a school or college is unable to offer benefits to the community it is guesting in, then it has no right to be tolerated.

20 **Stuckism embraces all that it denounces. We only denounce that which stops at the starting point—Stuckism starts at the stopping point!**

Billy Childish
Charles Thomson
4.8.99

theories, and tactics Bruce Mau shares in his 1998 *Incomplete Manifesto for Creative Growth*, a blueprint that not only guides his design projects, but also inspires a counterintuitive approach to living life to the fullest with fearless abandon and visionary vitality.

OPPOSITE "Incomplete Manifesto for Growth," Bruce Mau, 1998.

Before settling into any sort of routine, try designing your day (your life) to support your artistic health and happiness. Trust your instincts, like those who adhere to the 1999 Stuckist Manifesto that sees painting as a medium of self-discovery. Stuckists believe you cannot refer to yourself as a painter unless you are painting every day. Do you have a daily practice?

In your manifesto brainstorm, you may think up clichéd philosophies and practices such as "push your boundaries" and "you don't need permission." Whether you summon a tried-and-true cache of trite concepts and cherished chestnuts, or tap into the expansive infinity of the collective unconscious, put a pin in the phrases and philosophies that resonate with you, because there are no rules.

In the course of creating your sacred document, ask yourself: "What do I stand for?" "What is art?" "Why is it important to me?" How will you honor your creative calling or crafty career? Consider your creative manifesto your pledge to yourself to honor the gifts you have been given: it is a map to keep you on track; a reminder to fall in love every day with your tools and materials, whatever they may be.

Examine your mind-set and reprogram the ideas and beliefs that don't serve you. There's nothing wrong with you, so just get going. You are 100 percent responsible for the results you get, so go and get them. Fill up your tank with inspirational and instructive podcasts, magazines, songs, books, and movies. Visit museums, travel, read, and enjoy life, making sure your manifesto articulates your ultimate commitment to creativity.

BRUCE MAU

incomplete manifesto for growth

1. ALLOW EVENTS TO CHANGE YOU
You have to be willing to grow. Growth is different from something that happens to you. You produce it. You live it. The prerequisites for growth: the openness to experience events and the willingness to be changed by them.

2. FORGET ABOUT GOOD
Good is a known quantity. Good is what we all agree on. Growth is not necessarily good. Growth is an exploration of unlit recesses that may or may not yield to our research. As long as you stick to good you'll never have real growth.

3. PROCESS IS MORE IMPORTANT THAN OUTCOME
When the outcome drives the process we will only ever go to where we've already been. If process drives outcome we may not know where we're going, but we will know we want to be there.

4. LOVE YOUR EXPERIMENTS (AS YOU WOULD AN UGLY CHILD).
Joy is the engine of growth. Exploit the liberty in casting your work as beautiful experiments, iterations, attempts, trials, and errors. Take the long view and allow yourself the fun of failure every day.

5. GO DEEP.
The deeper you go the more likely you will discover something of value.

6. CAPTURE ACCIDENTS.
The wrong answer is the right answer in search of a different question. Collect wrong answers as part of the process. Ask different questions.

7. STUDY.
A studio is a place of study. Use the necessity of production as an excuse to study. Everyone will benefit.

8. DRIFT.
Allow yourself to wander aimlessly. Explore adjacencies. Lack judgment. Postpone criticism.

9. BEGIN ANYWHERE.
John Cage tells us that not knowing where to begin is a common form of paralysis. His advice: begin anywhere.

10. EVERYONE IS A LEADER.
Growth happens. Whenever it does, allow it to emerge. Learn to follow when it makes sense. Let anyone lead.

11. HARVEST IDEAS.
Edit applications. Ideas need a framework, field, generative contstraint to make life manifestation. Use the other hand, benefit from critical rigor. Produce a high ratio of ideas to application.

12. KEEP MOVING.
The market and its operations have a tendency to reinforce success. Resist it. Allow failure and migration to be part of your practice.

13. SLOW DOWN.
Desynchronize from standard time frames and surprising opportunities may present themselves.

14. DON'T BE COOL.
Cool is conservative fear dressed in black. Free yourself from limits of this sort.

15. ASK STUPID QUESTIONS.
Growth is fueled by desire and innocence. Assess the answer, not the question. Imagine learning throughout your life at the rate of an infant.

16. COLLABORATE.
The space between people working together is filled with conflict, friction, strife, exhilaration, delight, and vast creative potential.

17. _____.
Intentionally left blank. Allow space for the ideas you haven't had yet, and for the ideas of others.

18. STAY UP LATE.
Strange things happen when you've gone too far, been up too long, worked too hard, and you're separated from the rest of the world.

19. WORK THE METAPHOR.
Every object has the capacity to stand for something other than what is apparent. Work on what it stands for.

20. BE CAREFUL TO TAKE RISKS.
Time is genetic. Today is the child of yesterday and the parent of tomorrow. The work you produce today will create your future.

21. REPEAT YOURSELF.
If you like it, do it again. If you don't like it, do it again.

22. MAKE YOUR OWN TOOLS.
Hybridize your tools in order to build unique things. Even simple tools that are your own can yield entirely new avenues of exploration. Remember, tools amplify our capacities, so even a small tool can make a big difference.

23. STAND ON SOMEONE'S SHOULDERS.
You can travel farther carried on the accomplishments of those who came before you. And the view is so much better.

24. AVOID SOFTWARE.
The problem with software is that everyone has it.

25. DON'T CLEAN YOUR DESK.
You might find something in the morning that you can't see tonight.

26. DON'T ENTER AWARDS COMPETITIONS.
Just don't. It's not good for you.

27. READ ONLY LEFT-HAND PAGES.
Marshall McLuhan did this. By decreasing the amount of information we lose room for what he called our "noodle."

28. MAKE NEW WORDS.
Expand the lexicon. The new conditions demand a new way of thinking. The thinking demands new forms of expression. The expression generates new conditions.

29. THINK WITH YOUR MIND.
Forget technology. Creativity is not device-dependent.

30. ORGANIZATION = LIBERTY.
Real innovation in design, or any other field, happens in context. That context is usually some form of cooperatively managed enterprise. Frank Gehry, for instance, is only able to realize Bilbao because his studio can deliver on budget. The myth of a gulf between "creatives" and "suits" is what Leonard Cohen calls a 'charming artifact of the past.'

31. DON'T BORROW MONEY.
Once again, Frank Gehry's advice. By maintaining financial control, we maintain creative control. It's not exactly rocket science, but it's surprising how hard it is to maintain this discipline, and how many have failed.

32. LISTEN CAREFULLY.
Every collaborator who enters our orbit brings with him or her a world more strange and complex than any we could ever hope to imagine. By listening to the details and the subtlety of their needs, desires, or ambitions, we fold their world onto our own. Neither party will ever be the same.

33. TAKE FIELD TRIPS.
The bandwidth of the world is greater than that of your TV set, or the Internet, or even a totally immersive, interactive, dynamically rendered, object-oriented, real-time, computer graphic-simulated environment.

34. MAKE MISTAKES FASTER.
This isn't my idea — I borrowed it. I think it belongs to Andy Grove.

35. IMITATE.
Don't be shy about it. Try to get as close as you can. You'll never get all the way, and the separation might be truly remarkable. We have only to look to Richard Hamilton and his version of Marcel Duchamp's Large glass to see how rich, discredited, and underused imitation is as a technique.

36. SCAT.
When you forget the words, do what Ella did: make up something else ... but not words.

37. BREAK IT, STRETCH IT, BEND IT, CRUSH IT, CRACK IT, FOLD IT.

38. EXPLORE THE OTHER EDGE.
Great liberty exists when we avoid trying to run with the technological pack. We can't dot the leading edge because it's trampled underfoot. Try using old-tech equipment made obsolete by an economic cycle but still rich with potential.

39. COFFEE BREAKS, CAB RIDES, GREEN ROOMS.
Real growth often happens outside of where we intend it to, in the interstitial spaces — what Dr. Seuss calls "the waiting place." Hans Ulrich Obrist once organized a science and art conference with all of the infrastructure of a conference — the parties, chats, lunches, airport arrivals — but with no actual conference. Apparently it was hugely successful and spawned many ongoing collaborations.

40. AVOID FIELDS.
Jump fences. Disciplinary boundaries and regulatory regimes are attempts to control the wilding of creative life. They are often understandable efforts to order what are manifold, complex, evolutionary processes. Our job is to jump the fences and cross the fields.

41. LAUGH.
People visiting the studio often comment on how much we laugh. Since I've become aware of this, I use it as a barometer of how comfortable we are expressing ourselves.

42. REMEMBER.
Growth is only possible as a product of history. Without memory, innovation is merely novelty. History gives growth a direction. But a memory is never perfect. Every memory is a degraded or composite image of a previous moment or event. That's what makes us aware of its quality as a past and not a present. It means that every memory is new, a partial construct different from its source, and, as such, a potential for growth itself.

43. POWER TO THE PEOPLE.
Play can only happen when people feel they have control over their lives. We can't be free agents if we're not free.

CREATIVE MANIFESTOS

CREATIVITY
TAKES
NO
EXCUSES

IF IT'S IMPORTANT ENOUGH,
YOU'LL MAKE TIME FOR IT.
IF YOU DON'T KNOW WHERE TO START,
START ANYWHERE.
IF YOU FEEL STUCK,
ASK SOMEONE TO HELP YOU OUT.
IF YOU'RE TIRED,
TAKE A TIMED BREAK.
IF YOU DON'T KNOW HOW TO DO IT,
TRY DOING WHAT YOU CAN.
IF YOU BELIEVE THAT YOU CAN DO IT,
YOU WILL.

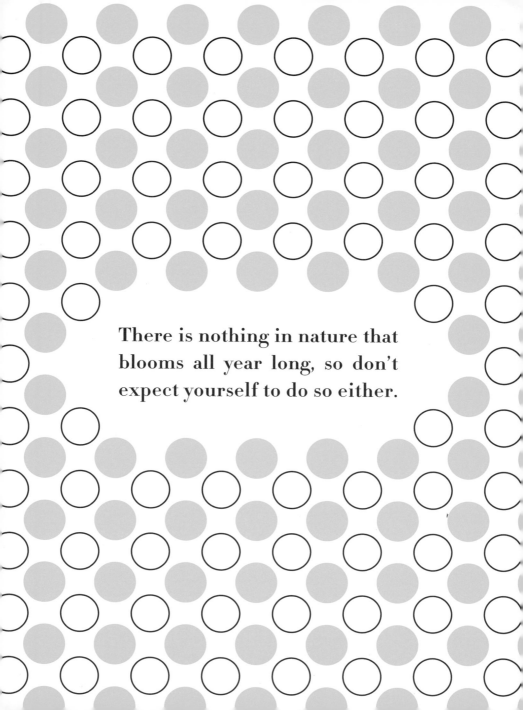

There is nothing in nature that blooms all year long, so don't expect yourself to do so either.

If I plan something

I never enjoy it as much,

I like the journey

of not knowing

how it turns out.

ART IS ONE OF
THOSE THINGS
WE SIMPLY MUST
DO SO THAT OUR
SPIRITS MAY

GROW

Be true to yourself and your profession.

Go offline: use a pencil, pen, and paper.

Be passionate about the work you do and show it.

Respect the past and help educate the future.

Never stop learning, never stop growing.

Use real typefaces from type designers and pay for them.

Don't let print die ... or film ... or letterpress.

Fill the world with beautiful design, not just more stuff.

Have real conversations, in person, over great coffee.

Move slower, take in the world, and get inspired.

Design for the past, the present, and the future.

Be honest, be humble, and be your best every day.

SUBJECTIVITY

The French-Cuban novelist Anaïs Nin believed, "We don't see things as they are, we see them as we are." Subjectivity—the idea that our preconceptions alter the way we perceive the world—is the foundation of the question *What is reality?* What do you see here? A handbag, a weight, a lock, a cupcake, a table and chair, or a man sitting in an armchair? Can you free your mind to make its own connections? If you can, you have the key to creativity and can unlock any door.

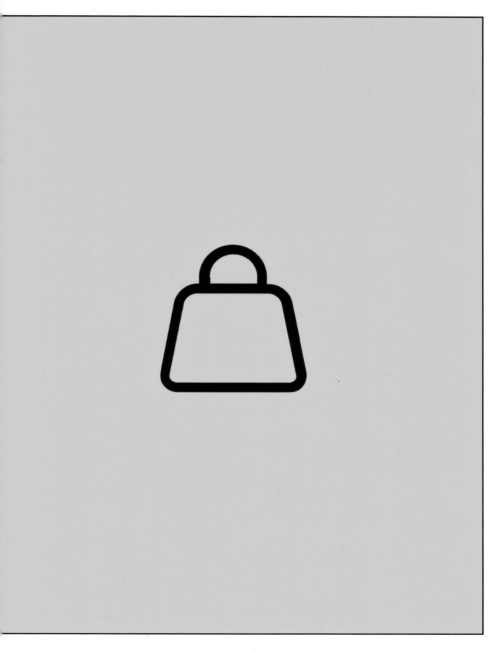

DESIGN

has a clear message

SIMPLICITY

is eye-catching

CREATIVITY

doesn't mean complexity

START

designing ready to restart

BE BOLD

visual communication is the bottom line

IT'S NOT ABOUT THE EXPENSIVE TOOLS—YOUR WILL TO CREATE IS WHAT ACTUALLY MATTERS.

SET A GOAL THAT MAKES YOU JUMP OUT OF BED IN THE MORNING.

THOSE WHO MOVE FORWARD WITH A HAPPY SPIRIT WILL FIND THAT THINGS WILL ALWAYS WORK OUT.

THERE'S ALWAYS A PERSON IN YOUR LIFE WHO APPRECIATES YOUR ART, EVEN WHEN YOU KNOW IT LITERALLY SUCKS.

THINK IT

WANT IT

GET IT

Forget the mistake, remember the lesson.

creating art gives

me an excuse

to get off

the beaten track

We are the League of Creative Interventionists.

We use art and culture as tools to reimagine the social and physical landscapes of our cities.

We believe that human connection is beautiful and necessary, and engaged communities are vibrant communities.

We create participatory spaces that invite connection and joy.

We are dedicated to catalyzing moments for equitable community transformation.

Whimsy is welcome.
Curiosity is crucial.
Listening is essential.
Love is an outcome.

SELF-DOUBT

According to the American writer Sylvia Plath, "the mortal enemy of creativity is self-doubt." Some of the most creative folks in the world lack confidence in themselves—or in their abilities—but overcome these paralyzing feelings by lending an ear to their inner critics and engaging in constructive conversations that often lead to new revelations about their work. Don't struggle to ignore or repress your self-defeating thoughts; instead, tune your dial to their frequency, listen to what they have to say, and write down what you hear.

16

HELPFUL TIPS TO BOOST YOUR CREATIVITY

1   Remember practice makes progress and a little progress is better than none.

2   Find one thing, no matter how small, that can you do today to keep the creativity flowing.

3   Leave a piece of work unfinished so you have a starting point for next time.

4   Create a space and vibe that enhances your creativity.

5   Stop copying or comparing yourself to others; it means you don't have belief in yourself and your capabilities.

6   Have inspiration on hand or pinned up for when you get stuck.

7   Remember "why" you create for times when you think you are "not good enough" and need the motivation to keep going.

8   Be open to new ideas and allow them to develop before discounting them completely.

9   If you start to feel uncomfortable or have fear of making a mistake, just sit with the feeling . . . it will soon pass.

10 When blocked or uninspired, go do something different, like visit a gallery or museum, work from a cafe, or walk in nature.

11 Guard your creative time zealously and make sure other people respect this, too.

12 Find time to be unfocused every day to give room for inspiration to visit and capture your ideas as soon as they come.

13 Be mindful of negative self-talk as it's fear holding you back in your comfort zone.

14 Make the experience playful as creativity is born from curiosity and play.

15 Forget about perfection as it stifles creativity and only leads to dissatisfaction.

16 Slow down, be present, and trust in yourself.

THERE'S NO GUIDEBOOK TO HAVING IDEAS

YOU SIMPLY HAVE TO SHOW
UP WITH A PURPOSE AND NOT
BE AFRAID TO BREAK THINGS

Start something small.
You can learn a lot about
how you work best
by doing small work.

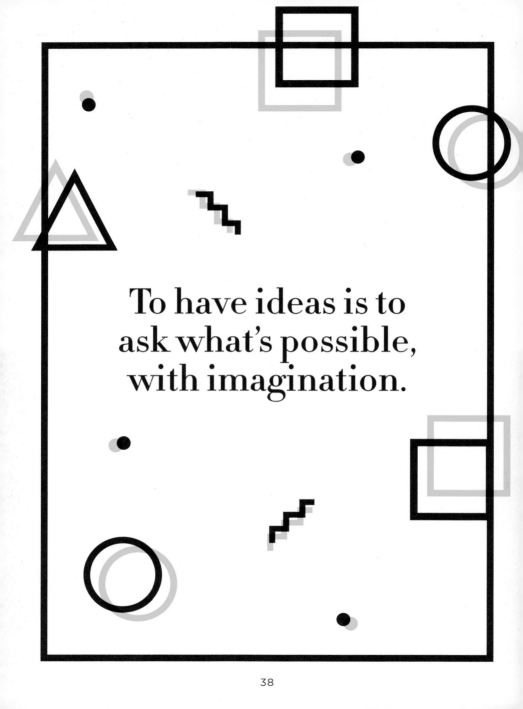

To have ideas is to
ask what's possible,
with imagination.

I DIDN'T COME THIS FAR
TO ONLY COME THIS FAR

PLAY

We know intuitively that creativity is what actor Mary Lou Cook describes as "inventing, experimenting, growing, taking risks, breaking rules, making mistakes, and having fun." What makes this approach to life, love, work, and leisure so essential is that there is no need to judge, analyze, or edit as you go. Rather, you give your inner child's innate curiosity free reign, time, a play space, and plenty of toys to play with. Sketch a scene incorporating the shapes provided. Don't think too hard about it—just see where your mind takes you.

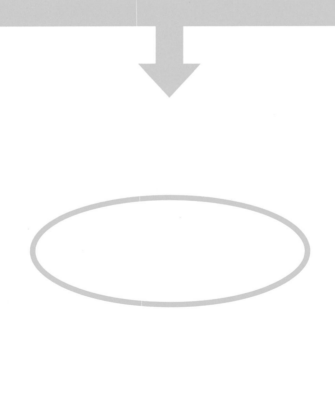

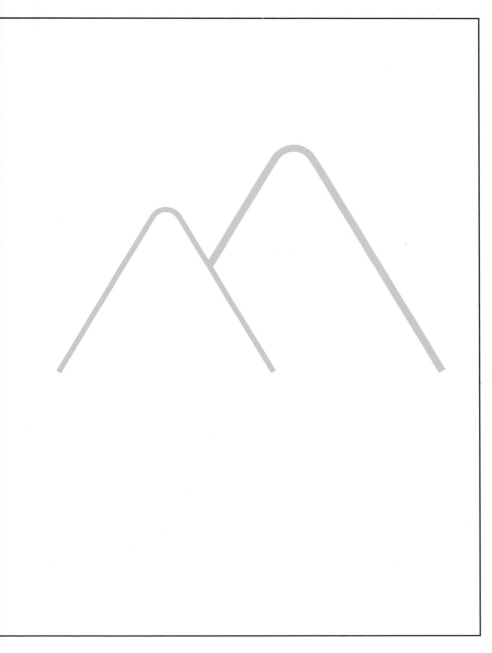

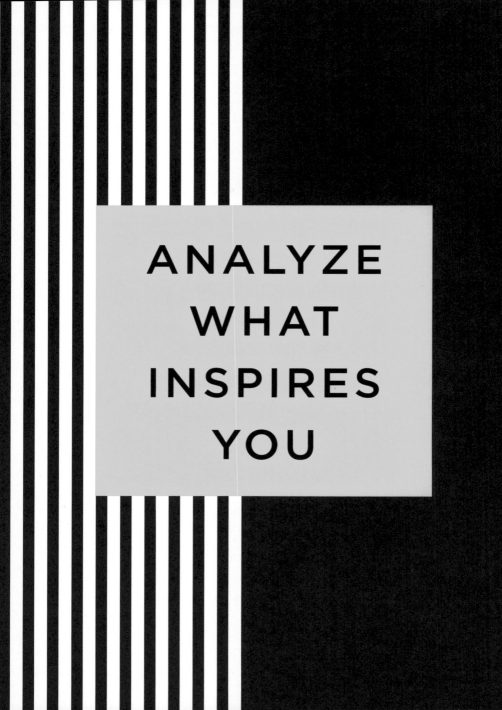

ANALYZE
WHAT
INSPIRES
YOU

OBSESSION

IS

ESSENTIAL

TO

CREATIVITY

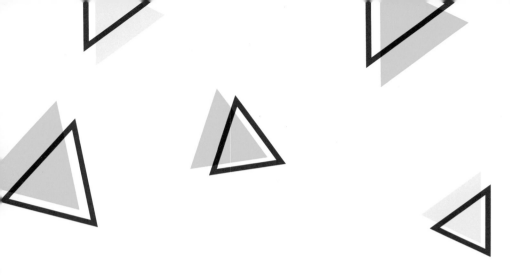

You can't teach creativity. No one can; and if they do,
it is artificial, hollow, fake. A type of creativity that
shouldn't exist, yet currently plagues the world in our
media and culture. Originality isn't even original today.
Our influencers are influenced by the influencers of
the past. So how can you create something original,
pure, and interesting? You have to find it yourself. Sure
there's various techniques, workshops, and other such
nonsense to help the individual to write, paint, or even
make a film—however, it's all detestable. Find your
voice, find your rituals, your own personal way to do
something. Personally, I cannot write, paint, or film
anything without strong drink, coffee (black), music,
and the room lit via neon lights. Years it's taken me to
figure out the routine that works for me; so at the end

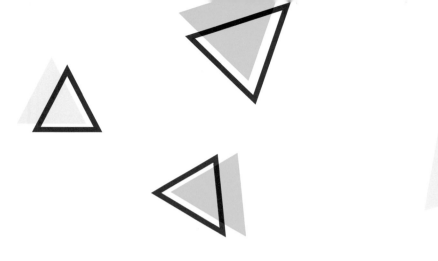

of it, when creativity has birthed some new, twisted window into my own dark and savaged psyche, I can say it is legitimately true, pure, raw, and completely untainted by some amateur greed in cheap money-making schemes. In all truthfulness, all forms of art are priceless, and that price is nothing. The ones that stick out and leave a legacy, that drop nukes of impact within society are the ones that represent the artist in their time and place of the world. No one knows in what our destinies lay. Still, some comfort should be had in knowing this: if your work brings a plethora of importance and satisfaction to you, what other acknowledgments should one really need? You are not a failure, only undiscovered. What's more exciting than undiscovered treasures?

21 ways to get creative

1 listen to music **2** spend time with children **3** people watch **4** read a book **5** take a walk **6** keep a journal **7** exercise **8** travel **9** take a break **10** take a shower **11** talk to a friend **12** turn the TV off **13** spend time in a garden **14** change your perspective **15** wander around a library **16** ask "why?" **17** get some sleep **18** clean a corner of your home **19** be open-minded **20** make a drawing **21** go on a local adventure

FIND WHAT
INSPIRES YOU.
THEN RECREATE
IT TO SEE HOW
IT'S DONE.

FIND WHAT
INSPIRES YOU.
THEN RE-CREATE
IT TO SEE HOW
IT'S DONE.

FIND WHAT
INSPIRES YOU.
THEN RECREATE
IT TO SEE HOW
IT'S DONE.

INTELLIGENCE

"Almost all creativity involves purposeful play," noted
American psychologist Abraham Maslow, best known for
his theory that we prioritize our needs in order of importance
on our trek to self-actualization. Climbing the ladder of
human evolution via creative expression will indeed yield
solace at the peak of the pyramid-shaped pinnacle of
his thesis. Remind your intuitive instrument that you are
über-intelligent, all-knowing, and have unlimited access
to super-playful universal energy. How will you harness it?
How do you like to have fun?

WHAT MATTERS ISN'T
NECESSARILY THAT
WE'RE MAKING THE
RIGHT STROKES, IT'S
THAT WE'RE MAKING
THEM AT ALL.

Be passionate

Life is too short to settle for less

Create great things

Make stuff that makes you proud

Share your ideas

And give creative credit to the one who deserves it

Be kind

Compassion brings happiness

Be brave

Find your way and believe in it

Make.
Help.
Smile.

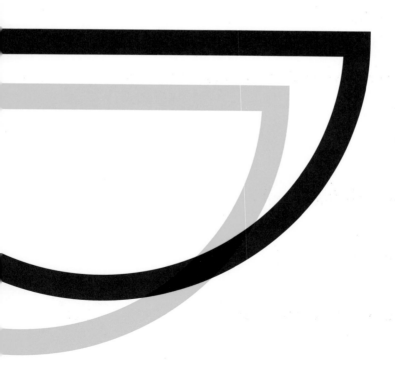

IDEAS AREN'T WORTH
ANYTHING WHILE IN
YOUR HEAD.

YOU HAVE TO GET
THEM OUT TO SEE
WHAT THEY CAN DO.

RULES OF A CREATOR'S LIFE

Try new things.

Teach others about what you know.

Do more than what you're told to do.

Make work into play.

Take breaks.

Always be creating.

Work when others are resting.

Make your own inspiration.

Love what you do, or leave.

CONNECT THE DOTS

Apple cofounder Steve Jobs observed that creativity is just connecting things: experiences, thoughts, elements, particles, ions, molecules, atoms, quanta—and in his case—software and hardware. What dots do you connect when you create something new? Do you see connections where others don't? What materials and methods can you fuse, attach, affix, and fasten to other components or substances to spark new ideas that lead you to innovative breakthroughs? Use the dots in the squares provided to draw your own creatures —there are infinite possibilities.

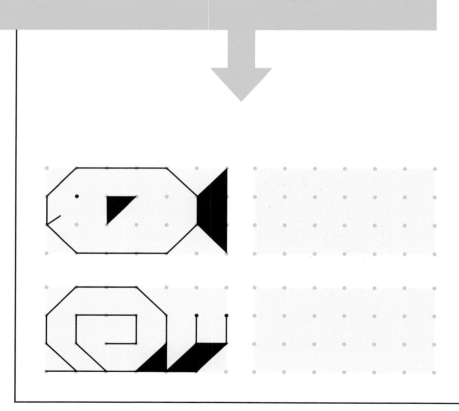

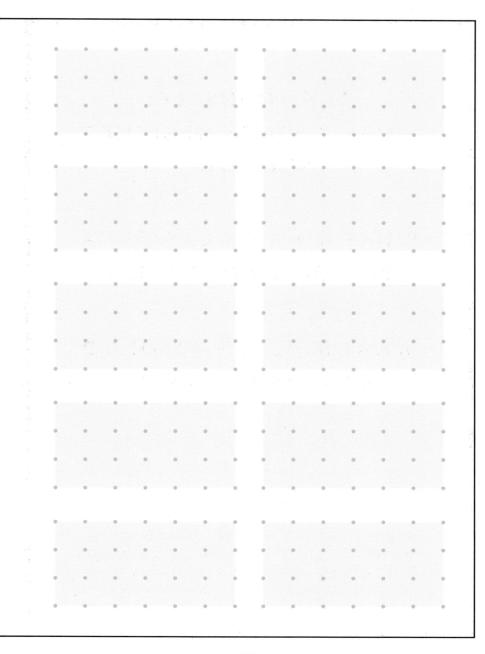

ASK YOURSELF:
WHAT KIND OF DESIGNER ARE YOU?

WHAT KIND OF DESIGNER DO YOU WANT TO BE?

WHAT KIND OF WORK DO YOU WANT TO DO?

IF YOU DON'T HAVE A SINGLE ANSWER, THEN MOST LIKELY, YOU ARE A DESIGNER. WHAT DEFINES YOU AS A DESIGNER SHOULD NOT BE THE SPECIFIC DESIGN SUB-DISCIPLINE THAT YOU USE TO SOLVE A SPECIFIC PROBLEM, BUT THE AREA(S) WHERE THE PROBLEM ARISES FROM.

your sense

of wonder

is an art form

DANCE SING

LAUGH **PLAY**

IMAGINE

FOCUS

LOVE

DREAM LARGE

CREATE

COMPLETE

WORK

How We Process the Visual and Create Something Unique

Sources of inspiration

YouTube

Museums

Social media

Classes

Pinterest

People and the world

We tie together the threads and add our own experiences and perceptions to create something unique.

WE ALL NEED A WELL TO DRAW FROM.

CREATIVITY IS A BREATHING EXERCISE.

"ARTIST" IS A PERSONALITY TYPE, NOT A JOB DESCRIPTION.

MAKERS GOTTA MAKE.

LIFE SHOULD BE BOTH ARTFUL AND ART-FILLED.

EXPERTS KNOW THE VALUE OF BEING A BEGINNER.

ART IS THE SUM OF WHO YOU ARE, WHAT YOU
EXPERIENCE, WHAT YOU IMAGINE & WHAT YOU DO.

MISTAKES ARE OPPORTUNITIES TO REASSESS.

EVERYONE NEEDS A MANIFESTO.

**AND OH YEAH, COFFEE BREAKS <u>ARE</u> A VALID
BRAINSTORMING TOOL.**

MANIFESTO FOR A CREATIVE LIFE

Go with the flow / Find your form of self-expression / Search for inspiration / Create a space of your own / Surround yourself with beauty / Leave your comfort zone / Ritualize your practice / Challenge yourself / Look on the bright side / Balance doing and being / Get out of your own way / Learn and create every day / Remember it's okay to copy / Be mindful / Accept mystery / Seek new experiences / Make connections / Find your tribe / Value the process / Invest in good supplies / Simplify / Take time alone / Pay attention / Play

NO LIMIT

"You can't use up creativity. The more you use, the more you have," spoke the author and poet Maya Angelou, reminding you that your imagination is a bottomless wellspring of ideas and abilities that will never run dry. Seek not to conserve your proverbial water supply in fear of losing it, but dip your pail into the infinite ocean of resources—both tangible and intangible—that power your diamond-tooth saw of an imagination, enabling you to polish your diamonds to an even finer shine. What ideas have sparked your imagination lately?

TO GO

WRONG

IN ONE'S OWN WAY

IS BETTER THAN TO GO

RIGHT

IN SOMEONE ELSE'S.

I BELIEVE IN THE MAGIC OF

TELLING STORIES WITH PICTURES.

•

I BELIEVE THAT STORIES NEED NOT

BE CONFINED TO BOOKS, AND

SHOULD BE FOUND EVERYWHERE

THEY CAN BE ENJOYED.

•

I BELIEVE THAT WONDERFUL THINGS

CAN HAPPEN WHEN YOU SHARE

YOUR MAGIC WITH THE WORLD!

INHALE

CONFIDENCE

EXHALE

DOUBT

like wildflowers

you must allow

yourself to grow

in all the places

people thought

you never would

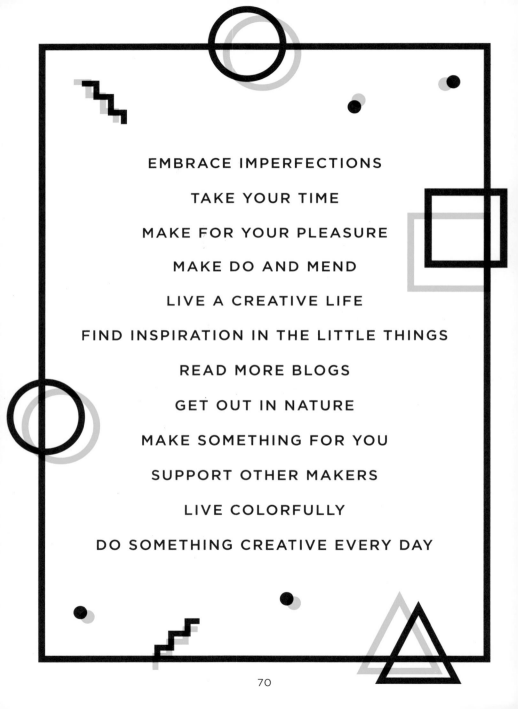

EMBRACE IMPERFECTIONS

TAKE YOUR TIME

MAKE FOR YOUR PLEASURE

MAKE DO AND MEND

LIVE A CREATIVE LIFE

FIND INSPIRATION IN THE LITTLE THINGS

READ MORE BLOGS

GET OUT IN NATURE

MAKE SOMETHING FOR YOU

SUPPORT OTHER MAKERS

LIVE COLORFULLY

DO SOMETHING CREATIVE EVERY DAY

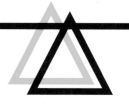

COLLABORATE

EXPLORE

LOVE WHAT YOU DO

EXPERIMENT

GO WITH THE FLOW

MAKE MISTAKES

LEARN A NEW SKILL

HOST A CRAFTERNOON

DON'T COMPARE YOURSELF

FOLLOW YOUR OWN PATH

GET OUT OF YOUR COMFORT ZONE

DO IT!

PERSPECTIVE

Once we have adapted to our environment, we have essentially conditioned ourselves to seek safety and security in the calm comfort of routine. These default settings running on autopilot help us avoid a variety of real and imagined threats, which keep us from designing and devising something new or renewing something old. But if we feel a deep desire to cocreate our lives, why not see like the great Leonardo da Vinci? He believed that "drawing is based upon perspective, which is nothing else than a thorough knowledge of the function of the eye." What do your eyes see that others don't?

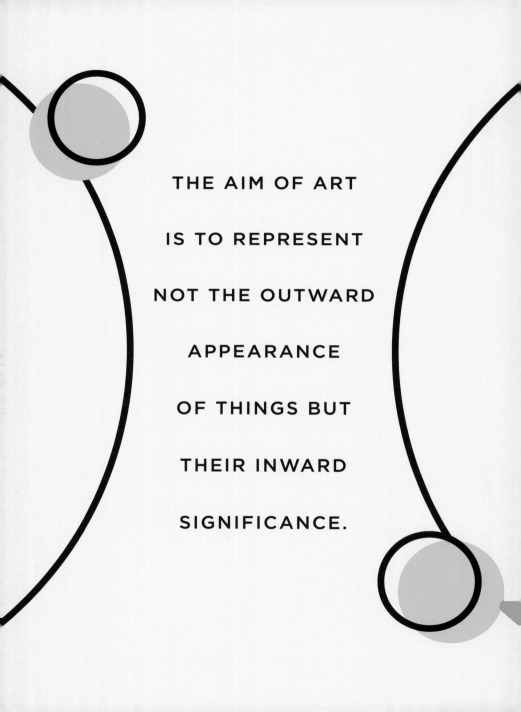

THE AIM OF ART

IS TO REPRESENT

NOT THE OUTWARD

APPEARANCE

OF THINGS BUT

THEIR INWARD

SIGNIFICANCE.

IT IS IMPOSSIBLE TO BE CREATIVE IN A VACUUM

Creativity. Messy. Imperfect.
Unpredictable. But always joyful.

~~~

Write for yourself. Write for others.
But never give anyone the privilege
to judge your work.

~~~

Don't let fear hold you back.
Fear lives in your mind, not in your heart.
The world needs the power of your heart.
The world needs your precious words.

~~~

Your writing is as unique as you are.
Stop trying to be something you're not and
allow your true voice to shine through.

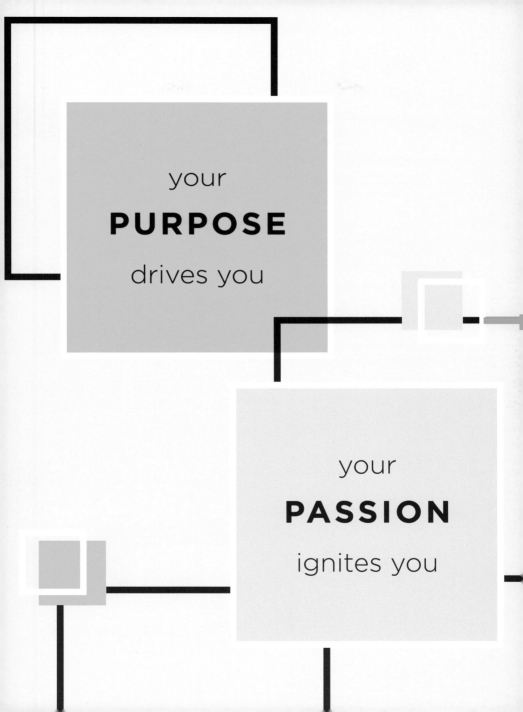

your
PURPOSE
drives you

your
PASSION
ignites you

WHAT CAUSES CREATIVITY .

1 CONFIDENCE
Ability to question without fear

2 OBSERVATION
Seeing problems and ideas

3 HUMILITY
Knowing you don't know everything

4 MINDFULNESS
Thinking on how to think

5 CURIOSITY
Exploring and experimenting

6 ENERGY
To explore and tinker

7 RESOURCEFULNESS
Something to tinker with

8 ACTION
Not just thinking but doing

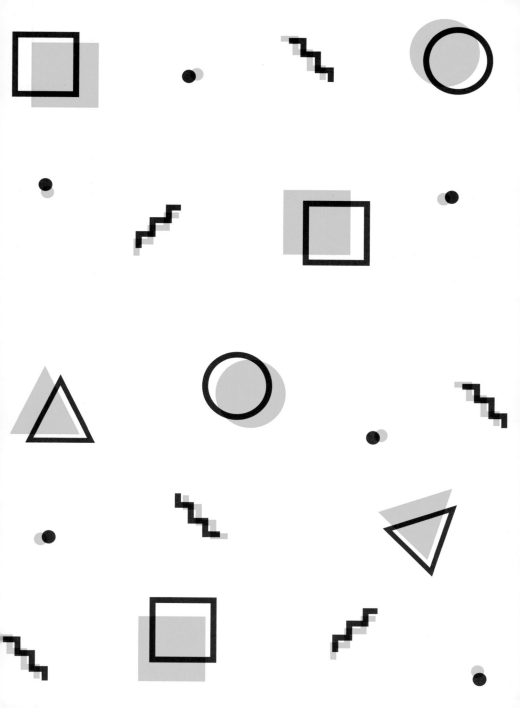

BALANCE

The convergence of abstract chaos and concrete order
is magic, which is similar to the American writer Dorothy
Parker's conclusion that "creativity is a wild mind and a
disciplined eye." What separates disorganized mayhem from
divine perfection? Only you can decide. Even when you find
the line, it is easy to cross it and quickly get lost in the woods
where every winding path seems to lead nowhere. When this
eventuality inevitably happens, go back to the basics. You
may think your life is a straight line, but it's probably not.
Draw it how it is, in the colors you see it.

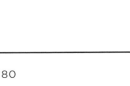

ALL THE CRITICS
IN THE WORLD

CAN'T STOP YOU
FROM CREATING
YOUR ART.

ONLY YOU CAN
DO THAT.

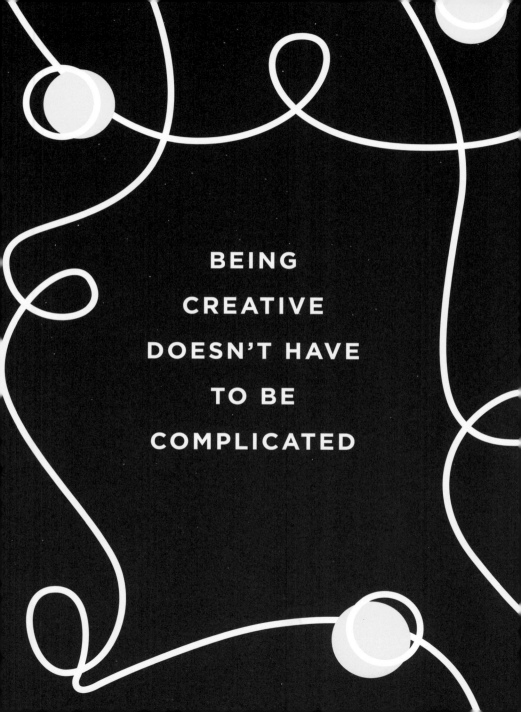

BEING
CREATIVE
DOESN'T HAVE
TO BE
COMPLICATED

An

ARTIST

is not paid for his

LABOR

but for his

VISION

CREATIVITY JUST TAKES CONFIDENCE
AND A LITTLE COURAGE. IT CAN BE
PRACTICED AND BUILT OVER TIME!

CREATIVITY JUST TAKES CONFIDENCE
AND A LITTLE COURAGE. IT CAN BE
PRACTICED AND BUILT OVER TIME!

CREATIVITY JUST TAKES CONFIDENCE
AND A LITTLE COURAGE. IT CAN BE
PRACTICED AND BUILT OVER TIME!

CREATIVITY JUST TAKES CONFIDENCE
AND A LITTLE COURAGE. IT CAN BE
PRACTICED AND BUILT OVER TIME!

CREATIVITY JUST TAKES CONFIDENCE
AND A LITTLE COURAGE. IT CAN BE
PRACTICED AND BUILT OVER TIME!

CREATIVITY JUST TAKES CONFIDENCE
AND A LITTLE COURAGE. IT CAN BE
PRACTICED AND BUILT OVER TIME!

CREATIVITY JUST TAKES CONFIDENCE
AND A LITTLE COURAGE. IT CAN BE
PRACTICED AND BUILT OVER TIME!

CREATIVITY JUST TAKES CONFIDENCE
AND A LITTLE COURAGE. IT CAN BE
PRACTICED AND BUILT OVER TIME!

THE
AI
MANIFESTO:

AS IF you could be disassembled into your constituent parts

AS IF you don't function as a whole

AS IF you are a calculating machine, pure reason, feeling nothing

AS IF you don't dream

AS IF you don't covet or consume yourself with petty jealousies. Turning your whole world green

AS IF you are not made of flesh and blood, bleed when cut, scream in your sleep

AS IF you don't hallucinate, laugh, cry, mourn, lie, cheat, deceive. Plot your own course then abandon all. Feel plagued with self doubt, self grandeur, self will, lack of will

AS IF there are not some of your number who see and hear things that really are not there. Those that hear from the prophets, hear from the Gods, become Gods themselves

AS IF you don't delude yourself, deceive yourself, know what to think, not think at all, stop thinking sometimes, suspend and transcend

AS IF you were a machine . . .

AI can already appear to reason, dream, defy logic, hallucinate, respond, be self-aware, see into the future, feign emotions, feign intuition, feign consciousness, feign conscience, think for themselves . . .

YOU CAN DO IT FOR REAL . . . BE CREATIVE. NOW. TODAY. BEFORE IT'S TOO LATE . . .

TRY IT

"I can accept failure. Everyone fails at something. But I can't accept not trying" remarked the great basketball star Michael Jordan, who likely sunk even more three-pointers in his imagination using creative visualization than he did on the court. The point is to break down the (often self-imposed) boundaries of what you believe to be your limitations and try something new. There are no rules. Forget what you learned in school. Who knows what could happen? Maybe what's stopping you is you. What do you think are your limitations?

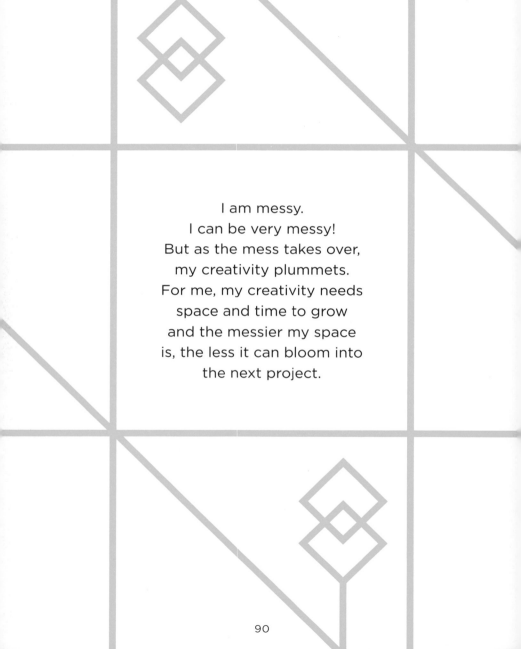

I am messy.
I can be very messy!
But as the mess takes over,
my creativity plummets.
For me, my creativity needs
space and time to grow
and the messier my space
is, the less it can bloom into
the next project.

THE MAIN THING IS

TO BE MOVED,

TO LOVE,

TO HOPE,

TO TREMBLE,

TO LIVE.

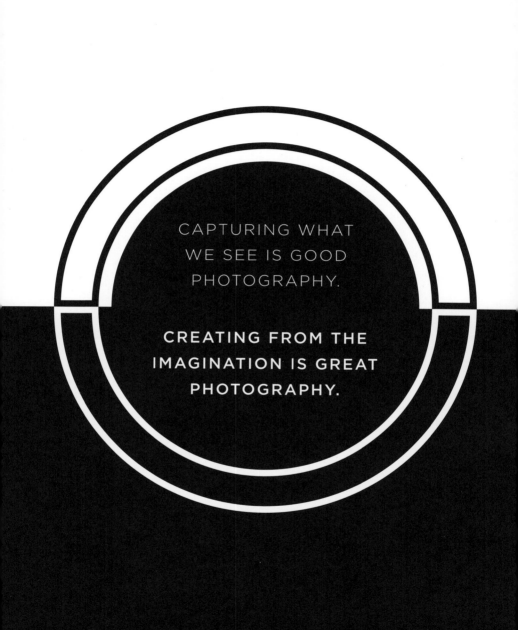

CAPTURING WHAT
WE SEE IS GOOD
PHOTOGRAPHY.

**CREATING FROM THE
IMAGINATION IS GREAT
PHOTOGRAPHY.**

CERAMICS HAS SO MANY

VARIABLES IT'S LIKE EXPLORING

A SERIES OF PANDORA'S BOXES.

JUST WITHOUT ALL THE WORLD'S

EVIL, INSTEAD THE OCCASIONAL

HAPPY ACCIDENT.

94

MAKE & MEND MANIFESTO

A STITCH IN TIME MENDS THE MIND

DO SOMETHING CREATIVE EACH DAY

BEAUTIFUL THINGS COME TOGETHER
ONE STITCH AT A TIME

MEASURE TWICE, CUT ONCE

EMBRACE YOUR FLAWS—STITCH THEM
TOGETHER WITH GOOD INTENTIONS

MISTAKES CAN BE UNPICKED

FINISHED IS BETTER THAN PERFECT

STITCH SLOWLY, BE PRESENT

HAPPINESS IS HANDMADE

SEWING IS GOOD FOR THE SOUL

YOUR FUTURE IS IN THE MAKING

LIVE COLORFULLY

THE ENEMY

Painter Pablo Picasso felt "the chief enemy of creativity is good sense," and you may see his belief demonstrated in his work. Playing with upside-down and inside-out portrayals of people and places, perhaps he was referring to the effects he felt by abstaining from the dangers of dreary convention, mind-numbing common sense, and typical thoughts when he was doodling in his sketchbook or mixing paint. What's the enemy of your creative process?

I _____ am a creative individual and curious spirit.

I was born to create art, write, sculpt, craft, collage, build, design, and share. I create for myself first, always making sure my creations speak to my own experiences, truths, and realities or honor the experiences, truths, and realities of others. I rejoice in the small creative projects like diary entries and homemade desserts. I equally rejoice in the bigger creative projects—the ones that contain an outpouring of my deepest fears, my anger, my power, and my heart. As I grow older, I continue to grow into my creative spirit, remembering that my creativity is a muscle that needs to be exercised regularly. Growing in my creative spirit is a continual re-birthing process; over and over again I am re-creating myself more open, more loving, more grateful.

My creativity is my freedom and my freedom is everything.

To find something you love to do is a gift.

To achieve recognition for it is a miracle.

THE CREATIVE YES COMES WITH SOME HARD NO'S TO SAY TO ANYTHING NOT ALIGNED WITH THE YES.

THE CREATIVE YES BREAKS OLD BOUNDARIES AND CREATES NEW ONES.

THE CREATIVE YES MEANS MORE LIFE . . . AND MORE RESPONSIBILITY.

THE CREATIVE YES CALLS YOU TO BE BIGGER, BOLDER, AND STRONGER.

THE CREATIVE YES BUMPS YOU UP AGAINST ALL THAT IS NOT YET THE YES IN YOU . . . AND THAT CAN SUCK FOR A WHILE.

THE CREATIVE YES MEANS COMMITTING TO NOT KNOWING.

THE CREATIVE YES MEANS THE STORIES AROUND THE NO ARE NO LONGER RELEVANT.

THE CREATIVE YES MEANS CLAIMING IT . . . EMBODYING IT . . . OWNING IT.

THE CREATIVE YES MEANS EMERGING MORE OF WHO YOU ARE OUT INTO THE WORLD.

THE CREATIVE YES DOESN'T JUST CHANGE WHAT YOU DO, IT CHANGES HOW YOU ARE.

THE CREATIVE YES

CALLS YOU TO BE

BIGGER

BOLDER

& STRONGER

THE 7 RULES TO UNDERSTAND DESIGN & DESIGNERS

1

Designers are meant to be loved, not to be understood.

3

The best designers are the ones who find the good clients.

2

The purpose of design is to make the ordinary extraordinary.

4

Design must seduce, shape, and more importantly, evoke an emotional response.

5

Good design can be planned but great design just happens.

6

Design the right things, design the things right.

7

Imagination is more important than knowledge.

SIMPLICITY

According to jazz legend Charles Mingus, "making the simple complicated is commonplace; making the complicated simple, awesomely simple, that's creativity." When people are bored—or simply unsure or unaware of their creative potential—they can't help but create confusion and muddle things up. Ever wonder why some of the most emotive, enchanting music is so simple? This is the gift of creative genius; it explains the inexplicable in an effortless way so the rest of us can comprehend it. How can you clarify your ideas into the simplicity of A-B-C and 1-2-3?

BE OPEN TO IDEAS

BE HAPPY AND KIND

BE GRATEFUL

PUT SOMETHING BACK

BE ACTIVE

DON'T JUST THINK ABOUT IT

CREATE ART THAT MAKES
PEOPLE STOP, LOOK, SMILE,
OR FEEL SOMETHING

ART IS IN

ALL THINGS

ALL THINGS

ARE IN ART

Art is not what you see,

but what you make others see.

THINGS I WISH SOMEONE HAD TOLD ME ABOUT **BEING AN ARTIST**

DON'T COMPARE YOUR WORK TO OTHERS.
COMPARE YOUR NEW WORK TO THE OLD.

YOU DON'T HAVE TO GO TO ART SCHOOL,
BUT DOING SO CAN GET YOU FURTHER, FASTER.

SOMEONE, SOMEWHERE, WILL LOVE WHAT YOU
DO (AND PAY FOR IT).
FIND THEM.

REALLY GOOD WORK TAKES A REALLY LONG
TIME TO MAKE.
BE PATIENT WITH YOURSELF.

CREATE EVERY SINGLE DAY.
**EVEN IF IT'S ALL GARBAGE, YOU CAN'T
IMPROVE ON A BLANK CANVAS.**

CHEERS TO BEING DIFFERENT—FOR THOSE ARE
THE PEOPLE WHO CREATE CHANGE IN THE WORLD

WHO LAUGH AT THEMSELVES AND INSPIRE CREATIVITY

WHO BELIEVE IN THEIR PASSIONS NO MATTER WHAT
ANYONE THINKS

THE PEOPLE THAT FEAR NOTHING ARE THE PEOPLE
THAT DETERMINE THEIR OWN FATE

SO BE BOLD—DREAM BIG AND DO THE IMPOSSIBLE

THE RULE BREAKERS BRING ENLIGHTENMENT TO
THE WORLD FOR THEY DON'T SETTLE FOR ONE
SOLUTION TO A PROBLEM

REMEMBER TO ALWAYS SIMPLIFY SIMPLIFY SIMPLIFY

BUT DON'T FORGET TO LOVE UNCONDITIONALLY
& NEVER GIVE UP!

I have been impressed with

the urgency of doing.

Knowing is not enough;

we must apply.

Being willing is not enough;

we must do.

BE WRONG

Joseph Chilton Pearce, author of books on human development, believed that "to live a creative life we must lose our fear of being wrong." If you are committed to creating something original, you will try things that will not give you the result you expected or wanted. Congratulations! Now you know one more way that doesn't necessarily give you the result you are after. Approach every attempt with the desire to learn, and let yourself test and risk and question everything. This is what separates the ordinary from the extraordinary. What risks are you ready to take in your work?

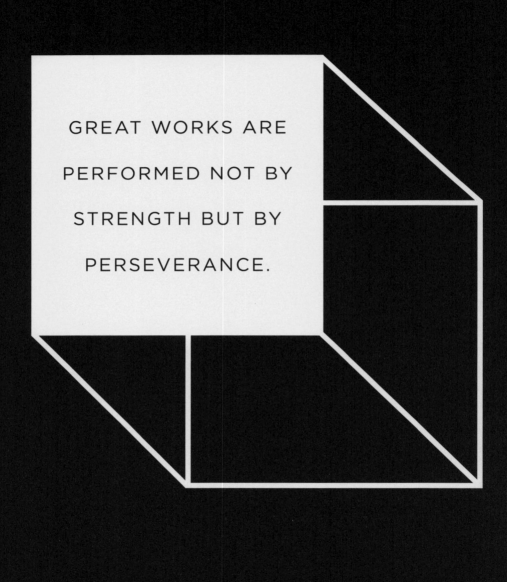

GREAT WORKS ARE
PERFORMED NOT BY
STRENGTH BUT BY
PERSEVERANCE.

ART IS TOTAL FREEDOM OF EXPRESSION.

LET YOUR SUBCONSCIOUS GUIDE YOUR
INTUITION INTO DOABLE IDEAS.

DON'T LIMIT YOURSELF TO "FINE ARTS" AND
ART CRITICS' IDEAS OF GOOD AND BAD ART.

GET COMFORTABLE WITH THE DISCOMFORT
OF BEING A STRANGER TO YOUR OWN ART.

BE OPEN TO THE WAYS YOUR ART CAN
MANIFEST AND GROW THROUGH NEW
AND MIXED MEDIAS.

I would rather die of

passion

than of

boredom

IF YOU HEAR A VOICE WITHIN YOU

SAY "YOU CANNOT PAINT,"

THEN BY ALL MEANS PAINT

AND THAT VOICE WILL BE

SILENCED.

SUCCESS

IS SOMETIMES THE OUTCOME
OF A WHOLE STRING OF

FAILURES

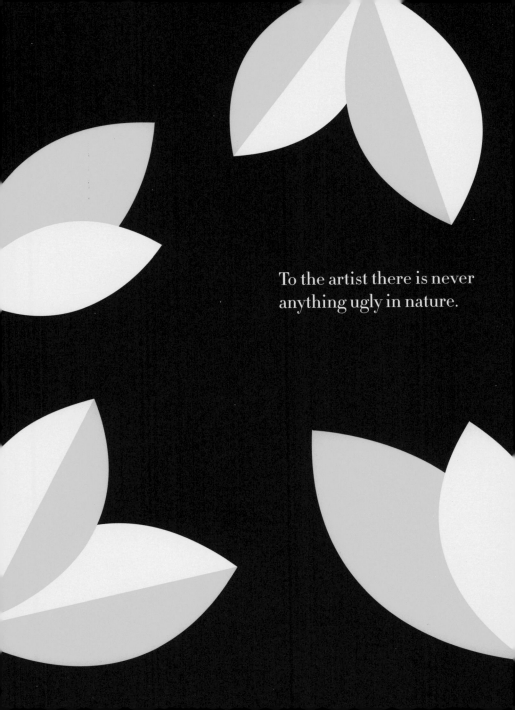

To the artist there is never
anything ugly in nature.

FREE YOUR MIND

Your mind moves at the speed of thought and experiences your environment with all its senses in every nanosecond you are alive. Designer Torrie T. Asai suggests that "creativity is nothing but a mind set free." So when you stop mulling over what to do and what not to do, what to say and what not to say, what to feel and what not to feel, and why you did or didn't do something, you will tap into your innate instincts and compose the sweet symphony of your life. So find a piano and play it. Stretch a canvas and paint it. Pick up a pen and express it. What's stopping you from freeing your mind?

I INVENT NOTHING, I REDISCOVER

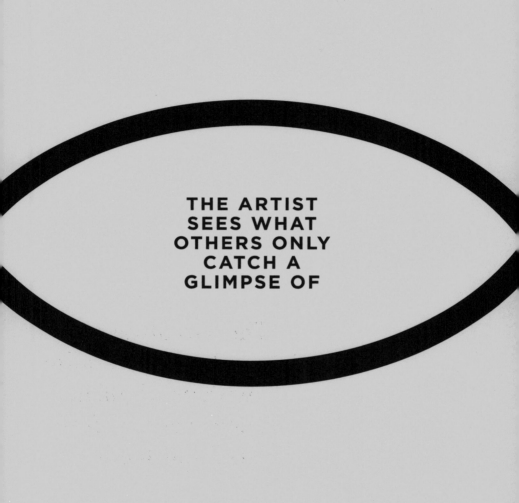

THE ARTIST
SEES WHAT
OTHERS ONLY
CATCH A
GLIMPSE OF

The part always has a tendency to reunite with its whole in order to escape from its imperfection.

I SAW THE ANGEL IN THE MARBLE AND CARVED UNTIL I SET HIM FREE

LIFE IS SHORT

ART IS LONG

Create every day

Dare to be different

Do it for love

Be kind to yourself

Finish what you start

PAINT YOUR DREAM

The Dutch painter Vincent van Gogh revealed a secret known by every artist since the dawn of self-expression: he would dream his painting and then paint his dream. Prior to the act of summoning something into existence, the creation is seen or felt or heard or sensed. The creative act begins by stirring the imagination and intuiting what form the whatchamacallit will take. Then come the ingredients: essence(s), material(s), and/or tools required are gathered to manifest the vision and make it real. What do you dream about?

MELISSA DINWIDDIE'S CREATIVE SANDBOX MANIFESTO

AKA THE 10 RULES I CREATED FOR MYSELF, THAT GOT ME OUT OF STUCK, PLAYING IN THE CREATIVE SANDBOX, AND LIVING A CREATIVE LIFE

FIRST AND FOREMOST, ALWAYS REMEMBER:

1 | THERE IS NO WRONG.

2 | THINK PROCESS, NOT PRODUCT.

4 | THINK TINY & DAILY.

"Ridiculously achievable." (Remember the most important practice is just getting back on the wagon. So it's a very good thing to make it a very short wagon!)

3 | THINK QUANTITY, NOT QUALITY.

If you take care of the quantity, the quality will take care of itself.

5 | IF YOU ARE STUCK, JUST START ANYWHERE!

(Yes, anywhere.) (I'm not kidding! This really works!)

6 | WHEN IN DOUBT: ASK, "WHAT IF...?"

7 | TAKE THE RISKIER PATH.

(When you know it needs something, but are afraid you'll ruin it? Go ahead & ruin it, baby! Worst case? You'll learn something!)

8 | DISMISS ALL GREMLINS.

9 | SPRING THE COMPARISON TRAP.

And most of all...

10 | TREAT YOURSELF WITH SWEET, LOVING, GENTLE, PATIENT COMPASSION.

Remember the golden formula: self-awareness + self compassion = the KEY to everything good!

NOW GO GET CREATING!

THE IMPERFECTIONIST

• MANIFESTO •

It's time to stop waiting because the universe needs you
to create!

Don't let perfect be the enemy of done.

Paint and paper is only wasted when it stays in the
tube or drawer.

You don't need to be good to have fun. So just start!
Anywhere! Now!

Ultimate value doesn't always have anything to do with
the technical skill.

Yes, the better you get, the more fun you can have,
But the more you let yourself be imperfect, the more stuff
you'll actually <u>do</u> and the better you'll get at it.

Allowing yourself to create crap doesn't mean you will
—it just means you'll create!

Remember: you need crap to fertilize the good stuff!

Let yourself be vulnerable, and share what you create:
putting stuff out in the world is really gratifying.

Even if you can't stand what you've created, you never
know how it may affect somebody else.

Other people and you see your work for what it is or
for what it isn't.

& above else: allowing yourself to be imperfect is just a
helluva more fun.

Prolificness = imperfectionism + effort + time
so make crap daily!

Photography does not begin and end with just a camera. Photography is more than the decisive moment; the flash, the snap, the shoot, or the touch. It is the moment of awe, the bewilderment, and the nostalgia that overcomes you and overwhelms you when you look at photography materialized into a photograph. We are subsumed into a culture that is entirely visual; we think, talk, touch, and see all through images. But not every image is a photograph. When you draw yourself into the shortest silence of a moment; when you hold up a camera close to your eye, your eye now one with that of the camera, a mechanical unity; think. Think just a little, before pressing, or snapping, or touching, the buttons or the shutters of your analogue, digital, or smartphone devices that have brought to you the experience of photography. Think about the moment that you will steal from the spatiotemporal continuum of life and preserve into the eternity of a photograph. Would this capture hold the ability to displace you from the present to the past, and then to your future? Is it something that you won't be able to prevent yourself from visiting and revisiting? If yes, then that is the power of photography. It removes you from yourself, and from the linearity of time. So open up the dusty doors of your archives and bring out the photographs that move you. Make photographs that will move you. It is time to experience and reactivate photography.

DOODLE

The wide world of webs can quickly wrap us up in its sticky silk and slowly suck the energy and attention span out of us like the spider who spun it in the first place. If you get stuck, do what American graphic designer Gerard Huerta suggests and "walk away from the computer and draw; it will teach you how to see." All you need to do to mix up a batch of this magical antidote is a pen or pencil and a piece of paper. Now doodle away, freely, and see what emerges.

I'M
AN ARTIST

I'M DONE WITH THE CONCERNS OF PLEASING OTHERS.

I'M DONE WITH THE CRITICS.

I'M DONE WITH STRIVING.

I'M PAINTING FOR MYSELF.

I'M SEARCHING AND FINDING MY WAY AS I PAINT.

I'M EXPLORING. I'M EXPERIMENTING.

I'M EXPRESSING ME.

A writer is someone who has taught his mind to misbehave.

THE EASIEST WAY TO BE CREATIVE

TRY SOMETHING
DIFFERENT

EVEN IF YOU DON'T THINK IT WILL WORK

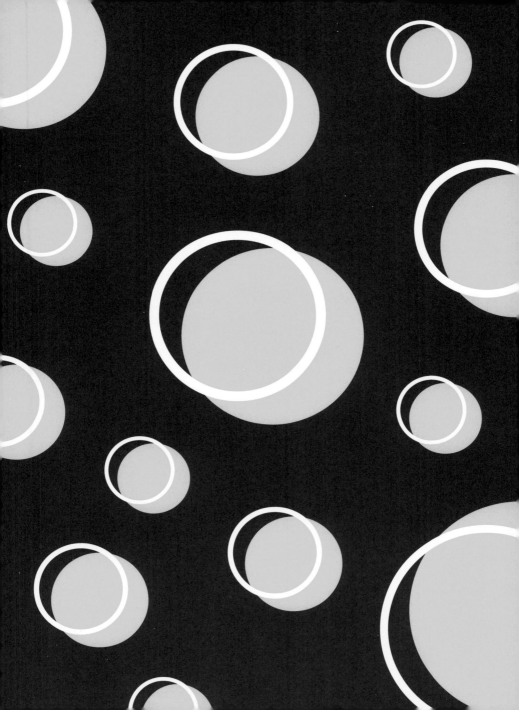

THE AMERICAN CRAFT COUNCIL MANIFESTO

We believe in a world where everyone is inspired to live a creative life.

We believe human beings are born to make things.

We believe making connects us all —in our families, our communities, around the world, and throughout history.

We believe that, in the modern world, making matters more than ever.

We believe tapping into our creativity shows us new possibilities.

Like our founder Aileen Osborn Webb, we believe a good life is found only where the creative spirit abounds.

We believe in the freedom to make mistakes, to fail, to learn, to grow.

We believe the history of craft is the history of what makes us human.

And we wonder: what will we make next?

INSPIRATION

Some poets note that lazying the day away under a tree for hours on end waiting for inspiration is the path to eloquent enlightenment, while practical creative professionals know that to make their dreams work, they have to agree with novelist and activist Jack London, who felt that you can't wait for inspiration; you have to go after it with a club. Thus, may you passionately pursue your muse and evoke eureka moments via any catalyst you choose. What are you chasing today?

I AM A PHOTOGRAPHER. I MAKE PHOTOGRAPHS. I DO NOT TAKE THEM, SHOOT THEM, CAPTURE THEM, OR SNAP THEM. I DO WHAT I DO TO SEE THE WORLD DIFFERENTLY AND TO SHOW OTHERS WHAT I SEE AND FEEL. AND YES, IT REALLY DID LOOK LIKE THAT WHEN SEEN THROUGH MY EYES, MIND, AND HEART. PROFESSIONAL OR NOT, I WOULD RATHER MAKE A PHOTOGRAPH LIKE AN AMATEUR DOES: FOR THE SHEER LOVE OF IT. THE TOOLS OF MY CRAFT ARE A CAMERA AND LENS. BUT THE TOOLS OF MY ART ARE MY PASSION AND VISION. FILM OR DIGITAL, IT'S NOT HOW WE MAKE OUR PHOTOGRAPHS THAT MATTERS, BUT THAT WE MAKE THEM. THE GEAR I HAVE IS GOOD ENOUGH. MY CAMERA DOESN'T HAVE TO BE MADE RECENTLY FOR ME TO PHOTOGRAPH THE PRESENT MOMENT. THE BRAND OF MY CAMERA IS IRRELEVANT TO THE PURSUIT OF BEAUTY AND AUTHENTICITY IN MY WORK. MEGAPIXELS ARE NO WAY TO MEASURE A PHOTOGRAPH.

I WANT DEEPER PHOTOGRAPHS: HONEST PHOTOGRAPHS THAT ARE ALIVE, NOT MERELY REALLY BIG OR REALLY SHARP.

I HOPE THE LEGACY I CREATE WITH MY WORK WILL BE JUDGED NOT BY HOW MANY PHOTOGRAPHS I MADE IN THIS LIFETIME, BUT WHAT THOSE FEW MAGIC FRAMES DO IN THE HEARTS AND MINDS OF OTHERS. COMPARING MYSELF TO OTHERS, OR THEM TO ME, IS A WASTE OF MY CREATIVE EFFORTS AND MAKES IT HARDER TO THE SEE THE LIGHT, CHASE THE WONDER, AND DO MY WORK. THERE IS TOO MUCH TO SEE AND CREATE TO WASTE THESE TOO-FEW MOMENTS. ART IS NOT A COMPETITION, BUT A GIFT. I BELIEVE PHOTOGRAPHS CAN CHANGE THE WORLD BECAUSE THEY HAVE DONE SO FOR ME. I BELIEVE PHOTOGRAPHY OPENS MY EYES TO A DEEPER LIFE, ONE THAT RECOGNIZES MOMENTS AND LIVES THEM DEEPER FOR BEING PRESENT IN THEM.

IF YOU TRULY LOVE NATURE, YOU WILL FIND BEAUTY EVERYWHERE.

A PAINTER SHOULD BEGIN EVERY
CANVAS WITH A WASH OF BLACK,
BECAUSE ALL THINGS IN NATURE
ARE DARK, EXCEPT WHERE
EXPOSED BY THE LIGHT.

I close my eyes

I breathe

I connect with myself

I create from that place

A DROP

OF ORANGE;

GET THE

CREATIVE JUICES

FLOWING

EXPERIMENT

Do you ever pull your ideas out of the garden of your imagination like weeds before they've even begun to sprout? Google cofounder Larry Page thinks that "if you're not doing some things that are crazy, then you're doing the wrong things." The world would be a very different place if he had tossed Google in the trash can before giving it a go. Dress up your sentimental duds and clunkers with a little attention before you let them dither and wither away in the snow. Into giants they may grow! What don't you know? Sing it, sculpt it, or draw it.

THERE ARE

NO MISTAKES . . .

JUST OPPORTUNITIES

FOR CREATIVITY.

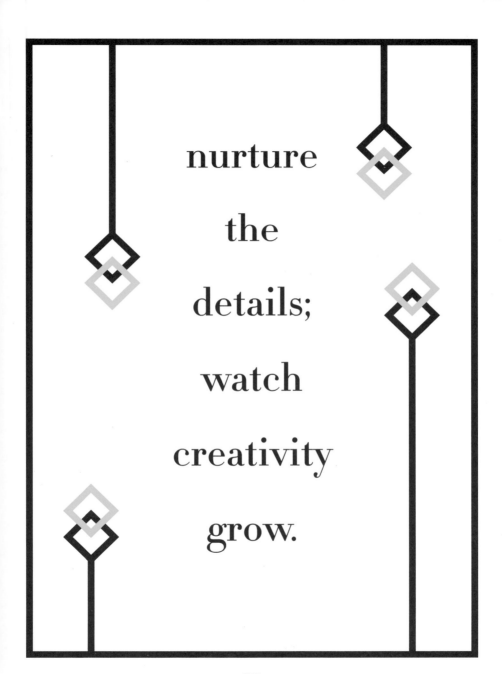

nurture

the

details;

watch

creativity

grow.

making

art

creates

peace

ART IS NOT A HANDICRAFT;
IT IS THE **TRANSMISSION** OF **FEELING**
THE **ARTIST** HAS EXPERIENCED.

I am a smarter artist

- I believe in my creativity, my brilliance, and my opportunity to succeed.

- A smarter artist makes all her decisions through the lens of her own unique purpose. She has a specific goal in mind. She works toward it every day. She knows her why.

- A smarter artist is smart as sh*t, but never strives to be the smartest person in the room. She surrounds herself with other smart people and isn't afraid to ask for advice or help.

- A smarter artist tries, she is always learning as she goes, and not everything will work out, but she knows it's not the end of the world. She is not afraid to fail.

- A smarter artist always stays true to who he is and never presents himself as something he's not. He is authentic and honest.

- A smarter artist rolls up his sleeves, and takes ownership of every step of writing and publishing, either doing the work himself or hiring smart people, but never abdicating or handing over career decisions to a gatekeeper.

- A smarter artist knows there's plenty of room for everyone, and that we'll all get better when we work together, giving, encouraging, and supporting each other along the way. He is always generous.

- I am getting smarter. I am getting better. I am building my career exactly as I want.

- I am a . . . smarter artist

The Creative Life is the authentic life.
It's releasing outdated assumptions and
beliefs that inhibit full expression.
It's following your aliveness.
It's cultivating the juicy richness that
is already inside of you.
It's saying yes to your uniqueness . . .
without apology.

LET IT BE

Surrealist artist Salvador Dali knew perfection wasn't possible, no matter what he attempted or accomplished. He said, "have no fear of perfection—you'll never reach it." How many countless hours/days/weeks/years have you spent in the pursuit of an elusive ideal? After a certain point, results decrease in proportion to the time, energy, and resources you have invested. The secret to (creative) success is knowing that not only does perfection not exist, but also when you have come as close to it as you are going to get. Use these pages to start something new.

If a person can maximize

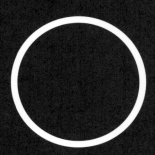

the ideas in her head,

the passions in her heart,

and the skills in her hands,

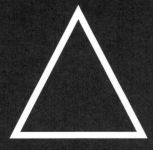

I think that results in the best work.

worry

stops

your

creative

flow

WITH CREATIVITY —————

————— YOU NEEDN'T

HAVE WINGS —————

————— TO FLY

BELIEVE

be*lieve

Believing in yourself is hard work.

No one can give that to you, it must be e a r n e d.

It requires the courage to try, to take chances to face your fears, and to give yourself a break when you screw up.

And you will.

It's the willingness to show up and accept the power you have to create the quality and course of your own life.

Most of all, it's believing you are worth believing in.

ARCHITECTURE IS ABOVE STYLE, IT HAS NO TASTE AND SHOULD RESIST SEDUCTIVE TRENDS.

SPACE IS SACRED—SOLID OR VOID, IT IS WHERE THE STORY UNFOLDS.

LIGHT IS OUR BUILDING TOOL, AS IS BRICK.

MATERIALS ARE INTRINSIC TO THE DESIGN PROCESS AND NEVER AN ADDITION.

CONTEXT IS IMPORTANT AND MUST BE CONSIDERED, YET IT SHOULDN'T BE RESTRICTIVE. HENCE WE PUSH AGAINST BOTH BLIND TRADITIONALISM AND CARELESS INNOVATION.

WE BELIEVE IN A HOLISTIC APPROACH VERSUS ISOLATION. CREATING A DIALOGUE BETWEEN THE OUTSIDE AND INSIDE, PRIVATE AND PUBLIC, SOLID AND VOID. EACH PROJECT IS CONSIDERED FROM TOP TO BOTTOM, SIDE TO SIDE, FRONT TO BACK.

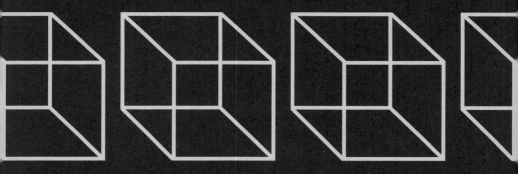

WE RESIST PURE AESTHETICISM IF DECONTEXTUALIZED AND UNRELATED TO THE SPACES WE BUILD. IMAGES AND DRAWINGS CAN BE LIMITING AND SHOULD ONLY HELP TO EXPLORE, EXPLAIN, AND AID THE BUILDING PROCESS.

WE UNDERSTAND INTIMACY AND ALLOW THEATER OF EVERYDAY LIFE.

WITH THE GROWTH OF CITIES AND THE RISE OF TECHNOLOGY, WE SEEK HUMANE AND ARTISTIC QUALITY IN EACH OF OUR PROJECTS, EXPLORING THEIR ABILITY AND POTENTIAL TO FURTHER THE RELATIONSHIP BETWEEN THE MAN-MADE AND NATURAL WORLD.

WE CELEBRATE NATURE AND ITS SCALELESS QUALITY.

OUR NOTES ARE BRICKS, OUR COLORS ARE WINDOWS, WORDS WRITTEN IN PASSAGEWAYS, COURTYARDS OF SYMPHONIES, TILED ROOFS OF HAPPINESS. THE BUILDINGS SPEAK TO US—THE STORY UNFOLDS IN THE CREASES OF THE EMPTY STREETS FAR FROM THE ILLUSORY IMAGES OF DESIRED TOMORROWS.

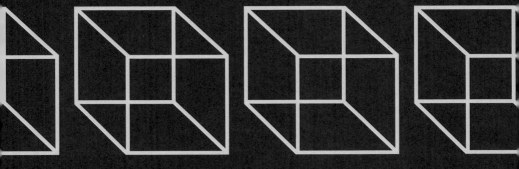

PATIENCE

Philosopher Ralph Waldo Emerson was convinced that "every artist was first an amateur." Everyone begins at the beginning, learning to walk and talk and read and write. You know that advancing toward achievement in any creative field is a step-by-step process. Sometimes it's two steps forward and one step back. Sometimes it's one step forward and two steps back. Find a coach or take a course and put your projects, programs, and performances through their paces. Patience and persistence always pay off. Draw what patience looks like to you.

WHEN I'M MAKING ART,

MY HEART BEATS FASTER

AND I FEEL JOYFUL.

Art is love.

The world needs your art.

The world needs your love.

Own your art: you are the only person in the world who can.

Stand up for it. Stand by it. Stand tall.

Show your love. Express your love. Represent your love.

Have faith that it matters. It does. Truly. Someone else, right now, is waiting for your art to appear, for their heart to be connected to yours, to feel that love, to feel understood.

Follow your imagination and instincts to a new kind of freedom.

Be courageous and curious.

Open your heart and trust your whole, living, breathing, loving self.

Trust your art.

Make art.

Make love.

One word away from
something special,
or one word away
from the mad house.

Either way they'll dress
you for the occasion.

So don't worry
and write naked.

MOTIVATED MASTERY

Your life will change when you change your mind.

Being stuck is a result of your fears overpowering your desires. Take the time to clean the lens through which you view the world; it will reveal what you missed.

Seek patterns and the meaning behind them. Do you chase happiness or do you create it?

Bravery is in high demand.

Curiosity is your greatest ally.

Don't be afraid to ask.

Sleep is not the cousin of death, excuses are.

A lot is learned by watching others.

Choose wisely who you're surrounded by.

Reinventing yourself helps you embrace your best, truest self.

Learn to enjoy discomfort.

Create the habit of falling forward; pick up the pieces, learn, and try again.

Access to knowledge and education is more available.

Harness this opportunity and help yourself.

In good times or bad, extract a lesson.

Failures forge heroes, not successes.

Make a difference, no matter the size.

Helping other helps yourself.

Every problem has a solution.

Anything worthwhile to your heart will elicit fear and self-doubt.

This is your cue to proceed.

No one can make you feel anything.

It is what you tell yourself that creates how you feel.

Yes, there are many broken systems in place. Stop complaining; use this obstruction not as an excuse to delay but to step forward and learn what others could not.

Everything that starts with you ends with you.

CREATIVE GODDESSES make art because it fills them up with joy and light.

CREATIVE GODDESSES believe mistakes are sacred and add to an artwork's story and perfection.

CREATIVE GODDESSES aren't afraid of making art that doesn't Look Good.

CREATIVE GODDESSES don't make art for others, they make art for themselves.

CREATIVE GODDESSES make art that is true for them.

CREATIVE GODDESSES don't need no stinkin' outside approval.

CREATIVE GODDESSES make art that doesn't need to look like anyone else's.

CREATIVE GODDESSES trust in their intuition and vision to make *their* art as it is needed in this world.

CREATIVE GODDESSES listen to their soul's calling.

CREATIVE GODDESSES dip their fingers in paint.

CREATIVE GODDESSES know the power of soulful creativity.

CREATIVE GODDESSES remember that every person on this planet is an artist, a creative spirit, a soul who needs love, joy, creativity, laughter, and connection just as much as water and food.

CREATIVE GODDESSES do it messy. And gladly. And reverently.

CREATIVE GODDESSES share their art when it is right for them, and hold on to the medicine of their art when it is right for them.

The CREATIVE GODDESS is inside you. She is inside each of us, everywhere, all the time. We only need a moment to hear our own grace and magnificence.

BE A REBEL

If you want to change the world with your creative work, take author Mike Sasso's advice. He reckons that "originality is the best form of rebellion." You can make a statement with your art, regardless of the medium. The flames of revolution and rebellion are often fueled and fanned by the efforts of the creatively minded among us. Even if your creative coup-d'état influences only a handful of colleagues or fellow students, believe in your power to inspire and empower all who come in contact with your work. Sketch out the most insurgent work lingering in your head.

1 If Architecture is to remain relevant as a discipline it must critically interrogate how it presents itself to the world.

2 In the age of consumption we must learn to consciously review the tools at our disposal.

3 We must be critical of our slavishness to the emergence of new technology, and be critical of tools it provides. The medium is, after all, the message.

4 We must remember that drawing is both a noun and a verb. We must fight against the dominance of the noun.

5 Architectural drawing is not, nor should it be limited to the tired triadic forms of plan, section, and elevation.

6 Conjectural drawings form a vital part of the development of new architectural paradigms and typologies.

7 A drawing (verb) is a palimpsestuous record of the process of turning tacit knowledge and intuition into an explicit form.

8 Drawing is not a finished thing, nor a singular moment, but something that develops and grows over time. Neither whole, nor complete, it offers the creator the opportunity for reflection and criticality, rather than endless speculative cogitation.

9 We must understand and exploit the plane of denotation's capacity to play host to heterogeneous ideas.

10 We must reject the limits of taxonomic convention and allow the manifestation of signifiers and must exploit the potential of their exchange.

I BELIEVE EVERYONE HAS

A CREATIVE SPIRIT AND

I LOVE HELPING OTHERS

EXPLORE THAT SPIRIT

NATURE ALWAYS REMINDS US THAT WE ARE ONE.

THERE ARE A MILLION WAYS TO FIND GRACE.

KNOW WHEN TO HOLD AND WHEN TO LET GO.

EVERY DAY WE ARE ASKED TO LISTEN WITH COMPASSION.

WALK THROUGH, NOT AROUND.

DREAMS COME IN ALL SHAPES AND SIZES.

FEAR CAN MAKE US NUMB. LOVE CAN MAKE US
FEEL EVERYTHING.

WE MUST OWN OUR OWN TRUTHS AND OUR OWN CRAP.

STORIES AND WORDS WILL FIND YOU, SOMETIMES WHEN YOU
LEAST EXPECT THEM. BE OPEN TO BEING FOUND. BE OPEN
TO BEING LOST, TOO.

GET MESSY. IT'S ALL BEAUTIFUL.

CHANGE IS NECESSARY IN ORDER TO GROW.

CREATIVITY IS A FORCE TO BE RECKONED WITH.
IT IS PURE ENERGY.
IT IS SACRED.
IT IS WHAT MOVES EVERYTHING FORWARD.
IT LEADS TO CHANGE.
LIKE A TREE WE MUST BEND WITH CHANGE.

BOOKS ARE PRECIOUS AND BEAUTIFUL; THEY TEACH YOU THINGS IN WAYS YOU CANNOT IMAGINE.

ART YOU CREATE WILL ALWAYS BE ABOUT WHO YOU ARE AND WHAT YOU WANT TO SAY.

TRUST WHEN THE PUZZLE PIECES DON'T FIT.

WE ALL SUFFER. TIME AND SPACE CAN HEAL EVEN THE GREATEST WOUNDS.

SPEND THESE PRECIOUS DAYS DOING WHAT BRINGS YOU JOY.

EVERYTHING BIG STARTS SMALL.

PASSION IS CONTAGIOUS.

MOMENTUM IS PART OF PASSION. FOLLOW THE THREAD.

NO ONE EVER FINDS COURAGE THE EASY WAY.

WE ALL MUST FIND OUR WAY BACK HOME, TO WHERE WE ARE ONE.

LOVE IS SIMPLE. CHOOSE SIMPLE.

GET COMFORTABLE WITH BEING UNCOMFORTABLE; SOMETIMES IT'S COURAGE IN DISGUISE.

OUR CREATIVE MANIFESTO

BE MINDFUL—
BY USING CREATIVITY TO BE PRESENT

USE OUR JOURNAL TO EXPLORE
AND EXPRESS YOURSELF

BE OUR CREATIVE SELF

BE INTUITIVE—
TRUST OUR CREATIVITY

PLAY

BE CURIOUS

BE INTENTIONAL IN OUR CREATIVITY

BE PRESENT WITH OUR CREATIVITY

HAVE FUN

STEER OUR OWN CREATIVE SHIP

NURTURE OURSELVES WITH CREATIVITY AS A SELF-CARE PRACTICE

COURAGE

The human race has survived because we are able to change, adapt, and grow. Beauty in all its forms would not exist if we remained safely tethered to shore, content only with what works. Believe that everything is broken and needs to be fixed. Renowned psychologist Erich Fromm suggests that "creativity requires the courage to let go of certainty." So jump and the safe and supportive net will appear (you aren't alone in your creative quest). What scares you the most?

CREDITS

p9 Futurist Manifesto *Manifeste du Futurisme*, Biblioteca Nazionale Braidense, Milan, Lombardy, Italy / Bridgeman Images

p10 The Laws of Sculptors, **Gilbert & George**, White Cube

p12–13 Stuckist Manifesto, **Billy Childish** and **Charles Thomson** 1999 [Billy Childish is an English painter, author, poet, photographer, film maker, singer, and guitarist. Charles Thomson is an English artist, poet, and photographer. Together, they named and cofounded the Stuckists art movement in 1999.]
Additional text from original manifesto to follow that reproduced on pages 12–13:
"The following have been proposed to the Bureau of Inquiry for possible inclusion as Honorary Stuckists:
Katsushika Hokusai
Utagawa Hiroshige
Vincent van Gogh
Edvard Munch
Karl Schmidt-Rottluff
Max Beckmann
Kurt Schwitters
First published by The Hangman Bureau of Enquiry, 11 Boundary Road, Chatham, Kent ME4 6TS"

p15 Incomplete Manifesto for Growth, **Bruce Mau**, Created by Bruce Mau Design

p18 Creativity Takes No Excuses, **Tanner Christensen** [Tanner Christensen is a digital product designer, author, developer, and entrepreneur working out of San Francisco, CA.]

p19 There is nothing in nature that blooms all year long . . . **Afke Warmerdam** [artist and illustrator]

p20 If I plan something I never enjoy it as much . . . **Lucy Levenson** [folk art designer and textile artist]

p21 Art is one of those things we simply must do... **Colleen Sgroi**, www.colleensgroi.com [artist, book illustrator and art teacher]

pp22–23 The Creative Manifesto 2015, **Kevin Zittle** [designer]

p26 Design Manifesto, **Kyle Berryman** [graphic designer]

p27 It's not about the expensive tools . . . **Anupama Thakur** aka Crafter Anu, www.instagram.com/handmadelove.ca [papercrafter and artist]

p28 Think it. Want it. Get it. **Minna So**, @minna_so, www.minnamay.com [multidisciplinary designer, illustrator, and creator]

p29 Forget the mistake, remember the lesson, **Minna So**

p30 Creating art gives me an excuse to get off the beaten track, **Helen Hallows**, www.helenhallows.com [mixed media artist and creative workshop leader]

p31 League of Creative Interventionists Manifesto, **League of Creative Interventionists**, www.creativeinterventionists.com [The League of Creative Interventionists sponsors projects that harness the creativity of local residents to create stronger, healthier, and more vibrant communities across the USA.]

pp130-31 Melissa Dinwiddie's Creative Sandbox Manifesto, © 2014 **Melissa Dinwiddie** [innovation strategist & creativity instigator]

pp132-33 The Imperfectionist Manifesto, **Melissa Dinwiddie**

pp134-35 Photography does not begin and end with just a camera . . . **Aayushi Gupta** [Aayushi Gupta is a researcher in photography at the University of Edinburgh, focusing on the philosophical, sociological, and cultural impact of photography, historically and amid the emerging trends of twenty-first century technologies.]

p138 I'm an artist . . . **Nancy Hillis** (to read Nancy's full Artist's Manifesto, visit nancyhillis.com/artists-manifesto) [Nancy Hillis is an abstract artist, author, and Stanford-trained existential psychiatrist]

p139 A writer is someone who has taught his mind to misbehave, **Oscar Wilde** [Irish playwright, poet, and writer, 1854-1900]

p140 The easiest way to be creative . . . **Tanner Christensen**

pp142-43 American Craft Council Manifesto, Reprinted with permission. American Craft, Vol. 77, No. 1, February/March 2017 by **The American Craft Council** craftcouncil.org/about-acc [For more than 75 years, the American Craft Council has championed craft. Our founder, Aileen Osborn Webb, recognized the significant impact craft has on individuals and communities, and established a nonprofit to preserve, cultivate, and celebrate this communal heritage.]

pp146-47 Manifesto, **David du Chemin** @davidduchemin davidduchemin.com [A world and humanitarian assignment photographer, bestselling author, digital publisher, and international workshop leader.]

p148 If you truly love nature you will find beauty everywhere, **Vincent van Gogh**

p149 A painter should begin every canvas with a wash of black . . . **Leonardo da Vinci**

p150 I close my eyes . . . **Helen Hallows**

p151 A drop of orange; get the creative juices flowing, **Helen Hallows**

p154 There are no mistakes . . . just opportunities for creativity, **Deborah Younglao**, www.deborahyounglao.com [abstract painter and jewelry maker]

p155 Nurture the details; watch creativity grow, **Helen Hallows**

p156 Making art creates peace, **Helen Hallows**

p157 Art is not a handicraft . . . **Leo Tolstoy** [Russian writer, 1828-1910]

p158 I am a Smarter Artist, **Sterling and Stone LLC**, sterlingandstone.net [story writers, publishers, podcasters, broadcasters, creative entrepreneurs]

p159 The creative life is the authentic life... **Michelle James**

p162 If a person can maximize the ideas in her head . . . **Deborah Boschert**, www.deborahsstudio.com [artist, author, teacher]